HOW TRICHA SAVED FAMILY FROM FIRE

Written by

J.S.Gahlaut

Illustrated by

Samuel

(An imprint of Clever Fox Publishing Pvt. Ltd.)

© Books Mantra
ISBN: 978-93-56486-03-4
All rights reserved. No part of this book may be reproduced or transmitted in any form by any means, electronic or mechanical, including photocopying and recording, or by any information storage and retrieval system except as may be expressly permitted in writing by the publisher.

(An imprint of Clever Fox Publishing Pvt. Ltd.)

Books Mantra
8 Sarva Space, 2nd Floor, SBI Bank Building,
Harinagara Cross Konankunte Post,
Anjanapura Main Rd, Bengaluru,
Karnataka 560062
www.booksmantra.com

Tricha, a **12** year old girl, and her 9 year old brother Trigya, lived in an apartment on the top floor of a **4**-storey building. She was a smart and intelligent girl. Trigya loved her sister and used to blindly follow her.

One day, as usual, both came home from school and finished their lunch with mother. Then they went to their room and started playing. Suddenly smoke started coming into the house from the staircase.

The thick and dark smoke was coming from the electric junction box which was installed in the staircase on ground floor.

Due to severe heat and smoke, the weak main door had collapsed and the smoke freely entered the house.

Tricha and Trigya got terrified.

Mother rushed to the children's room but could not see them. In the tense situation, she hurriedly presumed that children have already gone down. Mother then did a usual mistake. She went to her room, opened the almirah and started stuffing the cash and jewelry in a bag.

After the initial shock, Tricha regained senses and recalled what was told by the Fire Officer who had come few months back to her school to impart fire safety training.

She immediately became cool and calm and realized the mistake made by them. Then she followed the correct action to be taken in case of fire. She went to mother's room and loudly told her to leave behind cash and jewelry and go down immediately. All three then rushed to the staircase but by now the staircase had become completely smoke-logged. It was impossible to go down through the smoke. The house also became dark and even the balcony door was not visible. Tricha then asked her mother and brother to crawl by the side of a wall, on hands and knees, towards the balcony.

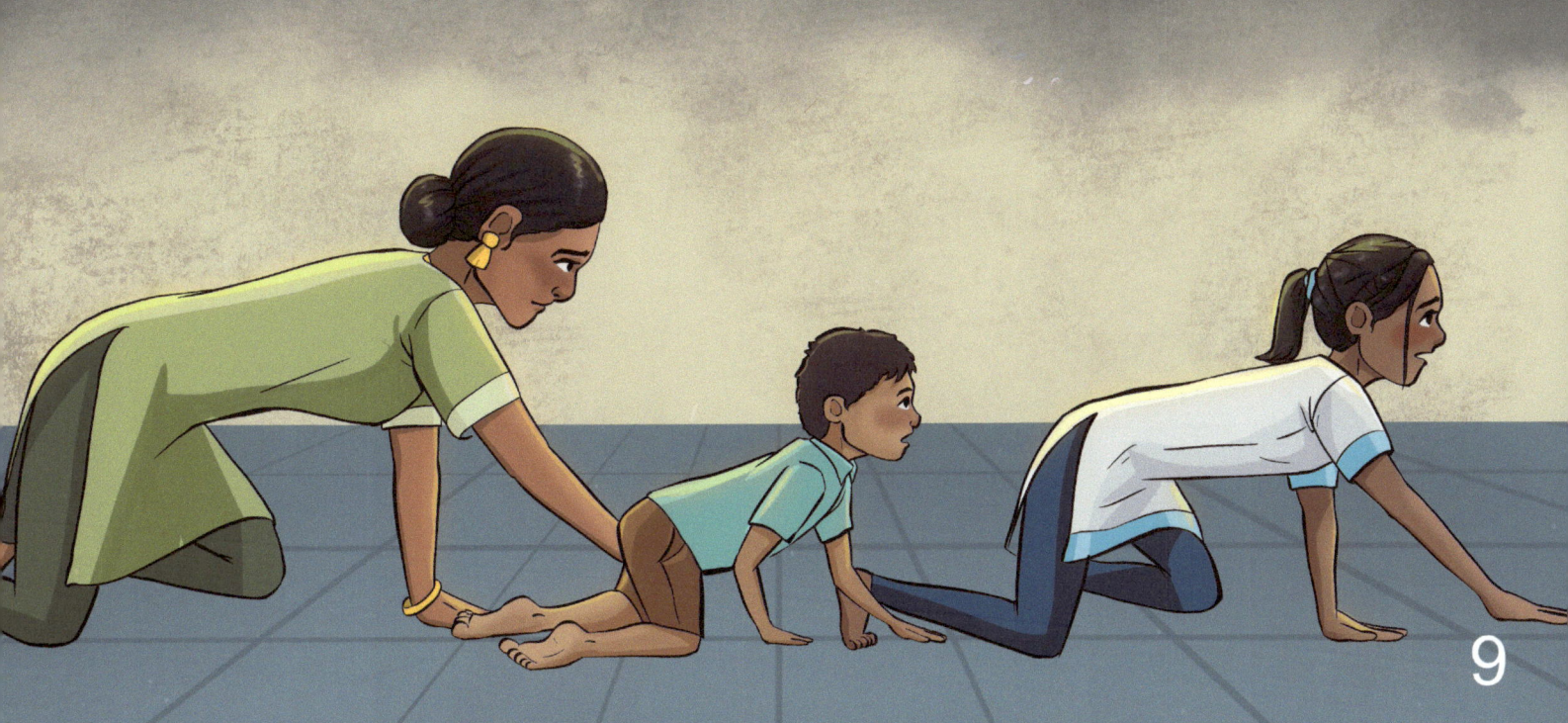

After reaching balcony, she closed the door, took out few clothes from the washing machine which was kept in balcony, and started stuffing them in the gap under the door to prevent smoke of house coming to the balcony.

Simultaneously, she asked her mother and brother to shout for help. Both shouted loudly but they were not heard due to traffic noise on the street. They then took out few more cloths and started throwing them on the people walking on road to draw their attention.

Soon many people gathered and someone from the crowd called the fire brigade. In a short while, the sound of blaring sirens was heard by all 3, which was like some extremely pleasant music never ever heard earlier.

The fire officer saw the mother and children trapped in the balcony. He immediately got the Extention ladder pitched under their balcony. He donned the Breathing Apparatus set and climbed the ladder along with other firemen who carried ropes with them.

On reaching balcony, while the fire officer consoled the children, firemen tied chair knots from the ropes. In a short time, all three got rescued slowly, one by one, on the chair knots.

By now her father had also rushed back from office and gradually all the family members recovered from the shock. Mother then narrated the whole story to everyone as to how Tricha saved their lives. On listening it, the young ladies from the crowd lifted Tricha on their shoulders.

When father asked her how she is so well informed, Tricha loudly told everyone that when a doctor, fire officer or a police officer comes to my school to create safety awareness, I pay special attention. I am confident that by being attentive, we can save our lives in case of emergencies and the efforts of government agencies will get fully utilized.

FIRE PRECAUTIONS
Do's and Don'ts

Do's

➤ In case of fire, remain cool and calm so that you can take correct decisions.
➤ Shout 'Fire, Fire, Fire' loudly to attract attention of others.
➤ Call the Fire brigade on 101 and Ambulance on 102/108. While calling, give full address with landmarks.
➤ Without taking any undue risk, try to use the fire extinguisher, if available in your building.
➤ In smoke-filled rooms, crawl to the nearest exit, by the side of a wall, on your hands and knees, and cover your nose with handkerchief.
➤ In case the clothing catches, stop where you are, drop to the ground, and roll, over and over, and back and forth, until the flames are out.
➤ Use normal buckets, which are available everywhere, to throw water on fires in curtains, furniture, clothes etc.
➤ In case of burns due to fire, oil, acid, etc., pour copious amount of normal tap water on burnt area and consult doctor.
➤ During the normal times, read the instructions written on the fire extinguishers. The method of operation, and suitability of different types of extinguishers on various types of fires, is written on each extinguisher.
➤ Install an 'ABC' type dry powder extinguisher in your home. It is suitable for extinguishing electrical and other general fires.
➤ Install Smoke detectors in your house. Most deaths, due to fire, occur at night when people are sleeping. Fire detectors awaken the people before they are overcome by smoke and toxic gases.
➤ While cooking, use tight-fitting clothes made from dense fabrics like khadi and denim. Use of an apron made of thick cloth can significantly reduce chances of a fire in clothes.
➤ Children must be forbidden from playing with matchsticks and lighters.
➤ Keep the children away from the burner, stove and hot objects. Best way to achieve it is to avoid bringing small children to kitchen.

- Handle cooking gas with utmost care. Liquefied Petroleum Gas (LPG) and Piped Natural Gas (PNG), both are highly flammable. However, PNG is comparatively safer.
- In case of gas fires, cut-off the gas supply.
- In case of fire in a frying pan, cover it with a bigger lid or wet towel or other thick wet cloth to smother the fire in the pan. Small frying pan fires can also be extinguished by throwing lots of baking soda or salt on it.
- Most of the fires are caused due to short-circuit in the electricity supply. Use ISI marked electrical items, like plugs, sockets, tube-lights, bulbs, geysers, heaters etc., to prevent many such fires.
- In case of electrical fires, cut-off the electric supply.
- Electric Main Switch should be mounted on a metallic box for greater safety against fire. A plywood box is prone to fires.
- Flickering tube-lights, hot plugs/ sockets, fuse getting blown frequently, frequent tripping of MCB etc., indicate some problem, which can result in short-circuit. Get it attended by an electrician.
- Maintain proper pest control to avoid rodent damage to electric wirings and equipments.
- Switch off the 'Electric Main Switch' when leaving home for a long duration.
- Apart from Diwali, fire crackers are used on many occasions. While using them always keep in mind the associated risk. Among all the fire crackers, most dangerous items are Flower Pots ('Anaar'), which cause maximum injuries, and the 'Rockets', which cause maximum fires.
- Use glasses or goggles while bursting crackers. In case sparks fall in eyes, pour normal water and consult doctor.
- In case of car fires, as soon as you sense the pungent burning smell or see the smoke, switch-off the engine and get out of the car.
- If the car doors get locked, use hammer to break open the window glass. In case hammer is not available, remove the headrest of a seat and break the window glass. The ends of the rods of headrest are made pointed for this purpose.

Don'ts

➤ Do not be under the impression that a fire will never occur in my home. In our country, more than 10,000 fires take place every year and many incidents in rural areas go unreported. Nearly 40 people die every day in these fire incidents.

➤ Do not hesitate to call the Fire brigade. There are no charges and no later problems what so ever.

➤ Do not use Lifts in case of fire because lifts may get stuck between the floors due to various reasons.

➤ Do not hide in wash-rooms, or below the bed, or behind almirahs. Children normally do this mistake.

➤ Do not remain in smoke-filled room for collecting cash, jewelry or other valuables.

➤ Do not go back into a burning building for any reason.

➤ Do not apply any cream, ointment or oil on burnt parts. Immediately use normal tap water

➤ Do not waste time in arranging blanket etc. to cover the person whose clothes have caught fire.

➤ Do not keep room heaters, puja lamps, incense sticks etc. near the curtains because they can blow over the hot objects and easily catch fire. As they hang vertically, the spread of fire is very fast.

➤ Do not throw water on electrical fires. It may cause severe shock. Water can be used after cutting-off the electric supply.

➤ Do not insert bare wires in a socket. Use proper plug.

➤ Do not throw flour on frying pan fires because it can explode and make the fire worse.

➤ Do not try to repair the burner or gas cylinder. Always let a qualified technician carry out repairs and replacements.

➤ Do not use lighted match stick or lighter to check gas leaks.

➤ Do not forget to turn-off the cylinder valve before going to sleep at night.

➤ Do not allow children to handle firecrackers without supervision.

➤ Do not drive recklessly while taking a burn victim to a doctor.

IMPORTANT INFORMATION

Apart from fire emergencies, please feel free to call fire brigade on telephone number 101 for various types of other emergency services.

The official motto of fire brigades in our country is:

We Serve To Save
"हम बचाने के लिए सेवा करते हैं"।

It means that the fire brigades are meant to serve and save the people in case of fire and many other emergencies such as drowning, house collapse, etc. They are trained and equipped for such emergencies. Not only humans, firemen serve and save birds and animals with equal urgency. Common examples are saving the trapped dogs and cats from a chajja, birds entangled in kite strings, lifting of bigger animals from wells.

SLOGANS

Slogans are succinct messages, capable of having a profound impact on our minds. Akin to images, slogans can change our attitudes and actions towards fire safety. Few fire safety slogans which have become extremely popular, due to their ability to stick in our minds, are given below:

1. Fire Is A GOOD SERVANT But A BAD MASTER.

2. If You Safely Play Your PART, The Fire Won't START.

3. Learn Not To Burn.

4. Fire Feeds On Careless Deeds.

5. Keep Fire In Heart, Not In Home

6. Always Keep In Mind- Cats Have Nine Lives, You Don't

7. TODAY'S Fire Can Ruin Your TOMORROW'S Plans

8. Children's Enemy – Curiosity Fires."

9. Fire PREVENTION Prevents Ashes Of DESTRUCTION

10. Be COOL To Fight HOT Fire

However, the most popular is Shakespeare's quote-

A little fire is quickly trodden out;
Which, being suffered, rivers cannot quench.

www.ingramcontent.com/pod-product-compliance
Lightning Source LLC
LaVergne TN
LVHW070443070526
838199LV00036B/691